Louisiana Sugarcane Pictorial

From the Field to the Table

Photography and Text
by
RONNIE OLIVIER

Ronnie Olivier

Acadian House
PUBLISHING
Lafayette, Louisiana

Copyright © 2014 (Photos and text) by Ronnie Olivier

All rights reserved, including the right to reproduce this book or portions thereof in any form whatsoever. For information, contact Acadian House Publishing, P.O. Box 52247, Lafayette, Louisiana 70505, or via e-mail: info@acadianhouse.com.

ISBN: 0-925417-93-9

- ♦ Published by Acadian House Publishing, Lafayette, Louisiana
   (Edited by Trent Angers; produced by Charlotte Huggins;
   map work by Robert Clements)
- ♦ Cover design and production by Glenn Noya, New Orleans, Louisiana
- ♦ Printed by Walsworth Press, Marceline, Missouri

Table of Contents

Preface 4

Introduction 5

   1. After 'grinding season' 7

   2. The work of early spring 15

   3. Planting and harvesting 25

   4. The milling process 43

   5. The refining process 61

   6. South Louisiana's sugar mills 66

   7. Images of the past 87

   8. Parting shots 92

Index 108

Acknowledgments 110

About the Photographer/Author 111

Preface

Getting it done with pictures

If a picture is worth a thousand words, then the 130-plus photographs in this book speak volumes about Louisiana's sugarcane industry.

Purposefully using a minimal amount of text, the photographer/author tells this story with an abundance of pictures he took over a 25-year period, illustrating many aspects of this hardy yet delicate agricultural enterprise.

He zeroes-in on scenes that are commonly observed by the public, as well as some that are seldom seen by anyone except those who work in the cane fields or in the sugar mills of south Louisiana. It's all here: The planting and harvesting of the crop, transporting it to the mill, the multi-faceted milling process, the storage of raw sugar, and the refinement of the sugar as the last step before it goes to the consumer's table.

The book also features rare, exclusive photographs of the 11 sugar mills that were in operation in 2014, plus nine others that are now closed. Likewise, the photographer presents a brief selection of images from a bygone era, as well as numerous spectacular shots of this modern, dynamic industry.

– Trent Angers
Editor

Introduction

Louisiana's sugarcane industry: The big picture

Sugarcane was introduced to Louisiana when French Jesuit priests brought the first stalks to New Orleans in 1751. Forty-four years later, plantation owner Etienne de Boré succeeded in producing granulated sugar from sugarcane, and the Louisiana sugarcane industry was born in earnest in the Crescent City in the winter of 1795.

From that point on, sugarcane plantations – many of them complete with their own small, primitive sugar mills powered by farm animals – began popping up along the Mississippi River in the New Orleans area. Then they began to appear along other major south Louisiana waterways, including the Red River, Bayou Teche and Bayou Lafourche.

For well more than two centuries now, sugarcane has been the livelihood of generation after generation of cane farmers and millers and those they employ. Through the years, more and more acreage was planted to cane, and technological advances made many aspects of cane farming more efficient and much less labor-intensive.

Still, this is an industry defined by seasonal routines: planting, cultivating, fertilizing, fighting insects and funguses, harvesting and milling. Then there are factors that are not within the farmers' control as they hope for a good market price per pound of sugar, wish for the right amount of rain, and pray that the crop is not ruined by multiple hard freezes or untimely hurricanes that can twist and flatten the cane and kill any chance of making a profit that year.

The grinding season ends when the new calendar year begins, and it is then that farmers start to get their fields and equipment back in shape for the next growing and harvesting season. Likewise, this is when mill owners and foremen see to it that their equipment is cleaned and repaired and that some of it is replaced.

When September rolls around, the harvest begins again as the cane is cut by mechanical harvesters, or combines – either the traditional whole-stalk cane-cutters or the more modern, more highly mechanized billet cane harvesters. Signs that the harvest is underway begin to appear as smoke rises from the burning fields and cane trucks and tractor-drawn carts full of cane are seen on the back roads and highways.

At the same time, the mills are cranking up and beginning their 24-hour-a-day, 7-day-a-week marathon that goes on for about four months.

The cane arrives at the mill and it is weighed, sampled for sugar content, offloaded, washed and pulverized before the juice is squeezed from it. The juice goes through various stages – heating, purification, evaporation and crystallization – before coming out as raw sugar.

The raw sugar is shipped to the refinery, where it is further processed to remove molasses, moisture, impurities and even its tan color. Then it is bagged for consumers or packagers or sent in bulk via train to food-processing companies.

After all is said and done, 20 percent of the sugar consumed in the U.S. comes from the cane fields of south Louisiana, where approximately 400,000 acres are planted to cane in 22 parishes. Some 17,000 people work in this industry. The state's 11 sugar mills process about 13 million tons of cane, and the industry's overall economic impact on Louisiana is an estimated $2.8 billion.

This vital industry and the people who work in it are recognized and even celebrated each year through the Louisiana Sugarcane Festival in New Iberia and the Sugar Bowl football game and related activities in New Orleans.

Even when the harvest is complete, farmers have a big job ahead of them: cleaning and repairing their tractors, trailers, carts and other farming equipment.

Chapter 1

After 'grinding season'...

(Mid-January through mid-March)

While the south Louisiana sugarcane industry is most visible to the public when it is in full swing in the fall, it is an industry that stays busy year-round with one activity or another.

The high point of the industry's activity is the harvest season, also called "grinding season," which runs from mid-September through December and often into early January.

Cleaning and repairing the farming and milling equipment

Immediately after the harvest is completed and the mills are finished grinding, another phase of work begins: the repair season. From mid-January through mid-March farmers are busy inspecting, cleaning and repairing all their equipment. Also, repairs to the sugarcane mills take several months, usually beginning in early February.

Wear and tear on harvesting equipment can be substantial, since farmers work to harvest the cane 12 to 14 hours per day, 7 days a week, for 3½ to 4½ months.

As cane farmers are tending to their equipment, cane millers are doing the same with theirs. During grinding season, the mills run 24 hours a day, 7 days a week, for 3½ to 4½ months. Once grinding is finished for the year, every piece of the mill's equipment is cleaned, taken apart, inspected and repaired or refurbished as needed.

Every electric motor, pump, turbine, fan, vessel, boiler and pipe must be inspected. Top-notch work in the maintenance and repair process – in addition to the installation of some new equipment – helps to assure that the next grinding season will run as smoothly as possible.

Repairing and refurbishing the fields

When the crop is being harvested, the continuous movement of tractors and other farm equipment up and down the rows and headlands will wear them down and tear them up. When this happens, the drainage system – which is designed to keep excess water out of the fields – breaks down and water collects in the rows. Excess water threatens the next generation of cane – the cane that will grow to produce new shoots for the beginning of next year's crop. Thus, after the harvesting season, the rows must be repaired and restored to prevent the new cane from rotting.

The headlands, too, must be restored to a smoother, flatter surface. The headlands – the earthen paths that surround the cane fields – serve as roads on which to drive the tractors, harvesters and trucks used in the farming process.

8 *Louisiana Sugarcane Pictorial*

Freshly cleaned cane-hauling trailers are lined up and ready for next year's harvest.

Tractors are a key part of sugarcane farming and must be kept clean and in good working order.

10 *Louisiana Sugarcane Pictorial*

When the grinding season is over, workers inspect large pieces of equipment that are central to the milling process. These two items, known as intermediate carriers, are part of the apparatus that moves cane from one mill unit to the next as juice is squeezed from the cane.

Rollers are lined up and ready to go back into service after being cleaned and refurbished following grinding season.

Welders fill in cracks that developed on rollers during the grinding season. Rollers such as these are components of the milling units that squeeze the cane.

'Burning the fields'

The most noticeable burning of the fields takes place during harvest season, right after the cane is cut. The shucks and leaves of whole-stalk cane are burned away while the stalks are lying across the rows. This extraneous material is burned because it is of no use in the milling process and, in fact, only slows down the process.

It's a different story with the shucks and leaves from cane that is chopped up and blown out into the fields by a billet harvester. Some of this material is burned shortly after the cane is cut, but the rest is left in the field and burned later, after harvest season. Then it is burned where it lies. Were it not burned, it would form a mat that would retain water and possibly cause parts of the next crop to rot.

A few weeks after the harvesting of the cane, farmers are busily at work preparing the fields for the next crop. **Above:** *A portion of the field is ploughed in preparation for replanting.* **Right:** *A ditch is made in the cane field to help with the necessary drainage.*

Smoke rises from a cane field as shucks and leaves on freshly cut whole-stalk cane are burned. With a whole-stalk harvester, the shucks and leaves are burned the day after the cane is cut. With the billet harvester, some of this material is burned right after the cane is cut and the remainder is set afire after the harvest season.

14 *Louisiana Sugarcane Pictorial*

Chapter 2

The work of early spring

In early spring, yellow flowers and various weeds can be seen taking over the sugarcane fields. This unwanted plant life – which uses up moisture and nutrients from the soil – is routinely killed off through the spraying of herbicides.

Insecticides are used to kill harmful insects that can damage the crop, and fungicides are sprayed to do away with funguses that sometimes appear on the cane.

Around this same time of year, the rows are re-worked. They are re-formed into the more raised shape that they were in before being eroded by rain and worn down by tractors, carts and harvesters moving through the fields during the harvesting season.

Then the rows of cane are fertilized. The fertilizer is usually applied directly onto the soil at close range to prevent it from being redistributed by wind or washed away by rain.

In early spring herbicides are sprayed to rid sugarcane fields of unwanted weeds.

Cane field rows are re-shaped in a process called off-barring, a routine springtime farming task.

Liquid fertilizer is applied to a young cane crop. The fertilizer is injected into the soil, rather than being sprayed on top of it, to assure it ends up exactly where intended.

Crop rotation

After cane has been harvested for three or four years in a row from the same fields, that land can be left fallow for 10 months or more, or an alternate crop can be planted there. The two most common such crops, soybeans and wheat, provide a nice supplement to the farmer's income.

A second reason for planting an alternate crop is that sugarcane fields require regular cultivation. Thus, the land and the weeds are kept under control – which reduces the work necessary to plant the next sugarcane crop.

Wheat is grown occasionally in place of sugarcane in some fields as part of a crop-rotation program.

Sorghum is one of the alternate crops grown in sugarcane's off-years.

Soybeans is the most common – and lucrative – alternate crop planted by cane farmers.

Tilling and re-applying herbicides

(Late spring)

From mid-May through early June, the fallow fields are plowed and shaped into rows into which new sugarcane crops will be planted, usually a couple of months later. The fields that are already planted to cane are also tilled and cultivated in late spring.

Also at this time, another round of herbicides is applied to the cane on an as-needed basis.

A cane field is leveled before rows are made for planting new cane.

Rows are formed in preparation for planting a new cane crop.

Herbicides are re-applied to maturing cane in late spring.

Insecticides and herbicides are sometimes sprayed from helicopters and airplanes.

Planting whole-stalk sugarcane by hand involves removing it from a wagon and laying it down on rows before covering it with soil.

Chapter 3

Planting and harvesting

(Late July through December)

In the summertime, while some fields of sugarcane are growing nicely and are maturing for the harvest in the fall, other fields are just now being planted and won't be ready for harvest for another full year.

Two ways to plant cane: Billets vs. whole-stalks

In late July through September, sugarcane that is tall enough is cut and used for planting new fields. This cane can be gotten from the farmers' own fields or bought from other cane farmers or from farms that specialize in what is called seed cane.

Two methods are used to plant cane.

One way uses a billet harvester and planter. The billets – which are segments of cane 12 to 30 inches long – are cut by the harvester, then mechanically planted into the rows by the billet planter. (The industry is moving gradually toward the exclusive use of this type of planting, as it is much less labor-intensive.)

The other way to plant cane is basically by hand. With this method, the whole-stalk cane is cut by a "soldier" harvester and loaded into a wagon. Then field workers take stalks of cane from the wagon and lay them down lengthwise in open rows and cover them with soil. Then the stalks are packed more tightly in the soil by a packer – which looks a lot like a set of 50-gallon drums being pulled behind a tractor.

Some farmers plant their cane using a mechanical whole-stalk planter. Here, too, a packer is used to secure the stalks in the soil.

A number of farmers heat-treat their cane before hand-planting it. This is done to help reduce or eliminate a certain bacteria that is known to stunt the growth of the cane.

This process entails cutting the cane, putting it in baskets, then submerging it in tanks of warm water (50 degrees C) for about two hours. The time and temperature are carefully regulated to kill the bacteria while at the same time retaining the cane's ability to germinate satisfactorily.

Workers position stalks of sugarcane on the rows. Next, the stalks will be covered with soil then pressed down firmly in the soil by the packer – the yellow implement in the background that resembles a set of 50-gallon drums.

Whole-stalk cane is loaded onto a mechanical cane planter wagon.

A mechanical whole-stalk planter plants cane without the use of hand-labor.

28 *Louisiana Sugarcane Pictorial*

A billet cane planter plants a new crop of cane in the peak of the summer.

Ripening the cane
(Late August to early September)

Between the end of August and early September, a ripening agent is applied to the mature cane that will be cut during the harvest season. The ripener is sprayed from a specially equipped helicopter or small airplane. The spraying continues usually until the first freeze of the season.

The ripener stops the sugarcane from growing further and essentially forces it to produce sugar; light freezes have the same effect.

A specially fitted plane sprays a ripening agent on nearly mature sugarcane a few weeks prior to harvest.

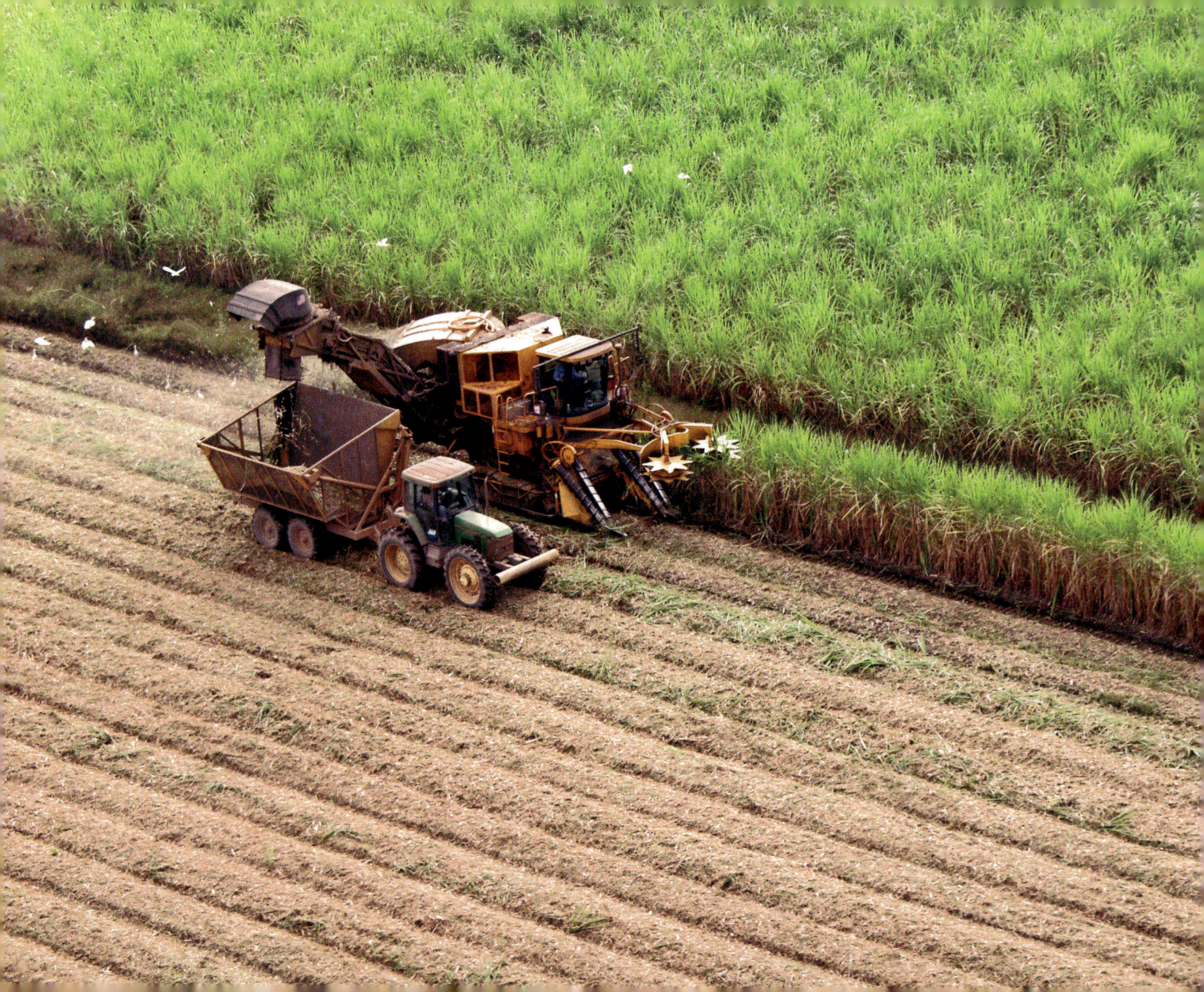

The harvest begins
(Late September to early October)

In late September to early October, the first cane that was sprayed with the ripener is cut to send to the sugar mill. Here again, it is either cut as whole stalks or cut into the shorter billets.

While the billet cane harvester cuts the cane, it also blows the majority of the leaves out into the field. This material will be burned eventually.

The whole-stalk harvester cuts the cane and lays it across the tops of the rows, perpendicular to the rows. The shucks are burned the next day or very soon thereafter – to prepare the cane to be sent to the mill for processing. The purpose of burning the shucks or blowing them into the fields with the billet harvester is to get rid of extraneous plant material that is of no further use in producing sugar. (The material that does make its way to the mill is ground up with the cane and slows down the milling process.)

The cut cane is loaded into carts and pulled to the mill by tractor, or it is dumped into 18-wheeler trucks for delivery.

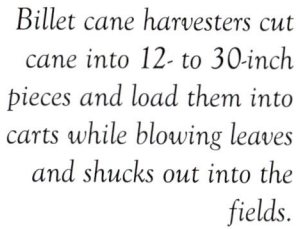

Billet cane harvesters cut cane into 12- to 30-inch pieces and load them into carts while blowing leaves and shucks out into the fields.

32 *Louisiana Sugarcane Pictorial*

Traditional whole-stalk harvesters, also known as "soldier" harvesters, cut cane and lay it down across the rows. This machine was the exclusive industry standard until the more highly mechanized billet harvester was introduced to south Louisiana in the 1980s.

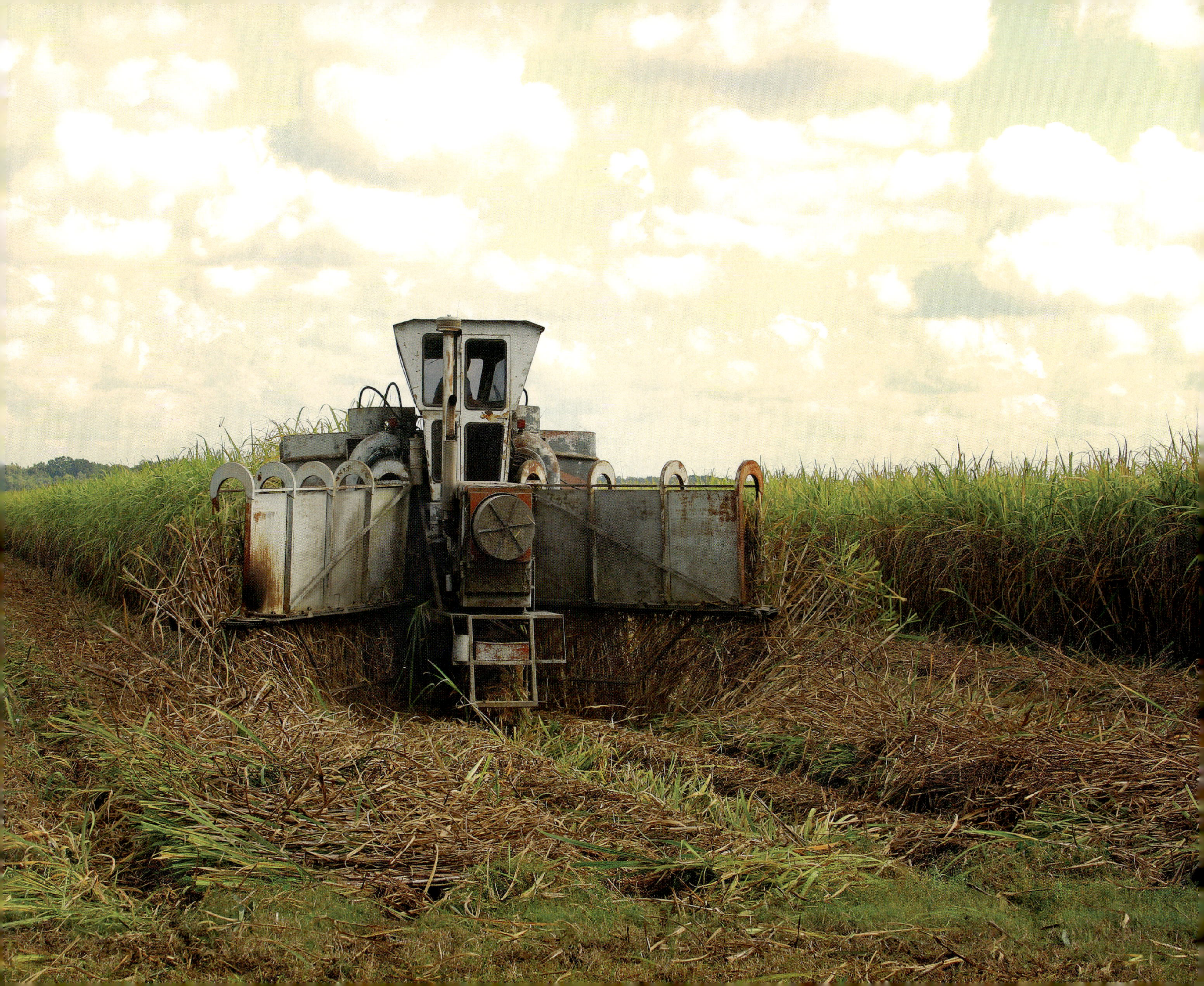

34 *Louisiana Sugarcane Pictorial*

When whole-stalk cane is cut and laid across the rows, farmers burn the leaves and shucks as a means of disposing of this unwanted organic material.

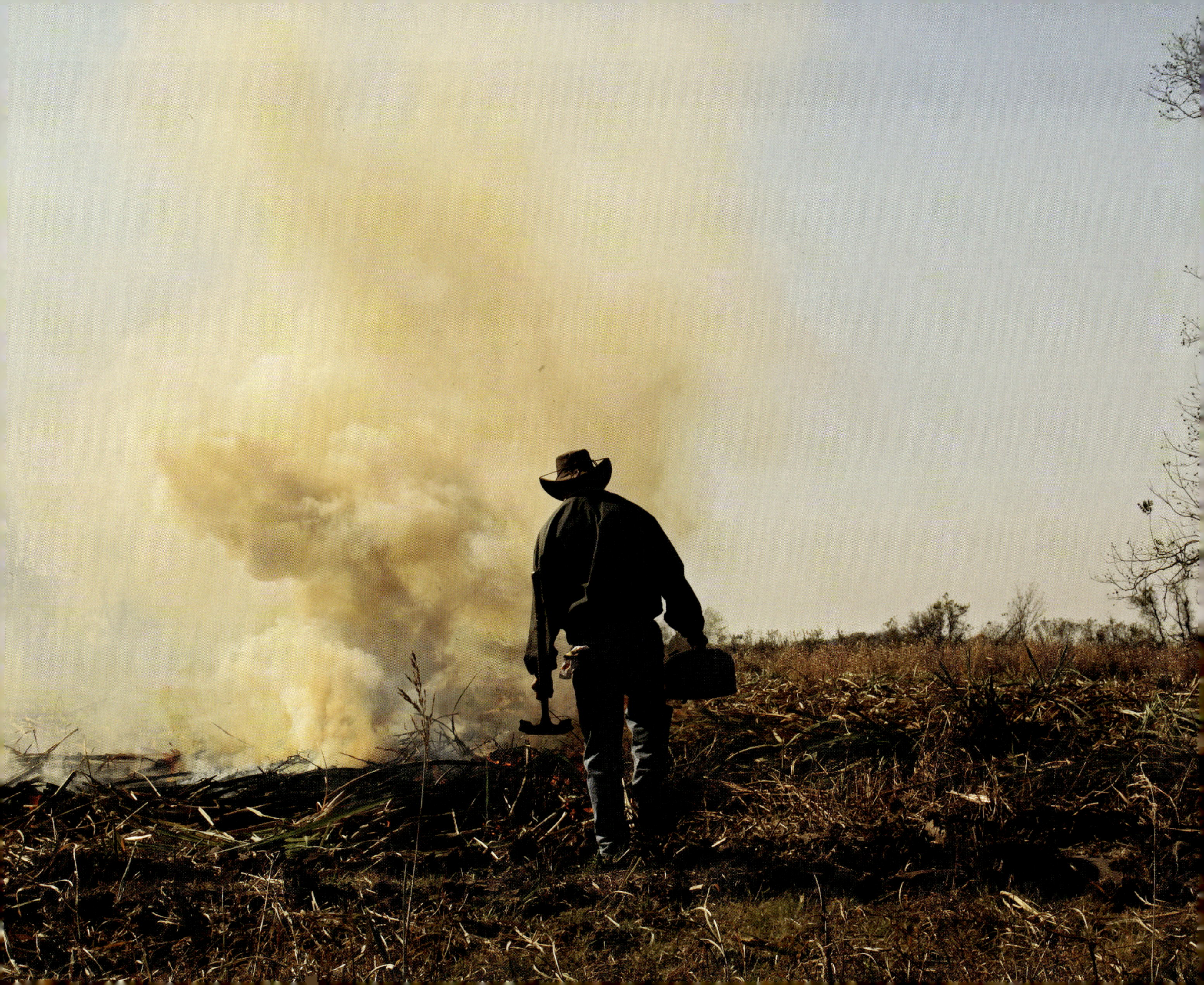

Smoke rising from burning cane fields is a common sight each fall in south Louisiana, and it has been for generations.

A cane field burns as whole-stalk sugarcane is loaded into carts that will take it out of the field.

A loader picks up sugarcane before moving it into a cart that will remove it from the field.

Cane is transferred from a cart to an 18-wheeler bound for the mill.

Tractors pull carts full of sugarcane out of a field. Nowadays the operator's cab on most tractors is fiberglass-encased to shield the driver from the cold and rain, but that wasn't always the case.

Eighteen-wheelers are a common sight on south Louisiana highways. **Above:** *A cane cart with a hydraulic lift dumps its load into one of the big trucks.* **Right:** *An 18-wheeler carries a heavy load of cane to a mill.*

A tractor pulls two carts of cane en route to a mill.

Sugarcane is weighed and sampled soon after the trucks and carts arrive at the mill.

◆ Weighing & Sampling

When the cane trucks and carts get to the mill, the cane is weighed while still in the trucks or carts to determine how much cane is being delivered.

The fully loaded truck and its payload are weighed when the truck drives up on a platform that sits on a below-ground scale. At this point, samples of the cane are taken and sent to the lab for testing. Then the cane is offloaded from the truck and the empty truck is weighed. The weight of the cane is the difference in the weight of the loaded truck and the unloaded truck.

Chapter 4

The milling process

The making of raw sugar from sugarcane involves a highly mechanized series of events that begin when the cane is delivered to the mill and ends just before the raw sugar is shipped from the mill to the refinery.

Cane is first weighed and sampled then offloaded from the trucks and carts. Then it is sometimes washed to rid it of as much mud as possible before being conveyed into the mill.

On the way in, the cane is chopped up and shredded then run through a series of rollers that squeeze the juice out of it. The juice is heated, clarified and then concentrated before being seeded with sugar crystals and spun with great centrifugal force to separate molasses from the mill's end product: raw sugar.

◆ Testing for sugar content

A sample of the cane is tested in the mill's laboratory to determine its quality – i.e., how much sugar there is in each ton of cane. The poundage of sugar per ton of cane is what determines how much the farmer is paid for the cane he delivers.

The mill's on-premises laboratory tests the cane to measure its sucrose content.

♦ Offloading

The trucks and carts are unloaded as soon as possible after their arrival at the mill – normally within 24 hours of when the cane is cut.

The cane is removed from the trucks and carts using one of several methods:

a) The truck is parked on a platform that is hydraulically lifted and tilted back at about a 45-degree angle. With this technique, called "end-dumping," the cane pours out of the back of the truck and onto a conveyor.

b) A forklift is used to remove two huge metal containers filled with cane from the bed of the truck; these containers are then emptied onto a carrier.

c) When carts are used, the carts are parked on a platform before being disengaged from the tractors that pulled them. The carts are locked down with cable and safety latches, then they are completely inverted, 180 degrees, and the cane is dumped into the cane yard.

d) The cart is pulled up to the outside wall of the cane yard, then a set of chains – which were pre-positioned in the cart – are used to lift the cane out of the cart. Some loads of cane are dumped directly onto the cane table, where it is washed to remove as much mud as possible as it makes its way into the mill.

A cane cart's load has been dumped directly onto the cane table, where it is washed to get rid of as much mud as possible before it is moved into the mill.

Two cane trucks are unloaded using a technique called "end - dumping" in which the trucks are tilted at a steep angle and the cane slides out the back and onto a conveyor. In the foreground, the cane in two carts is being dumped into the cane yard.

A cane trailer's payload is dumped onto the cane table.

◆ Moving cane into the mill

Cane in the cane yard is picked up by a grab and deposited on the cane table or sometimes directly onto the main carrier, or conveyor, which moves it into the mill. Front-end loaders are also used to place cane from the cane yard onto the cane table.

A giant-size grab picks up cane and moves it toward a carrier, which brings the cane into the mill.

Louisiana Sugarcane Pictorial 47

A front-end loader picks up cane in the cane yard and brings it to the cane table to be washed and moved into the mill.

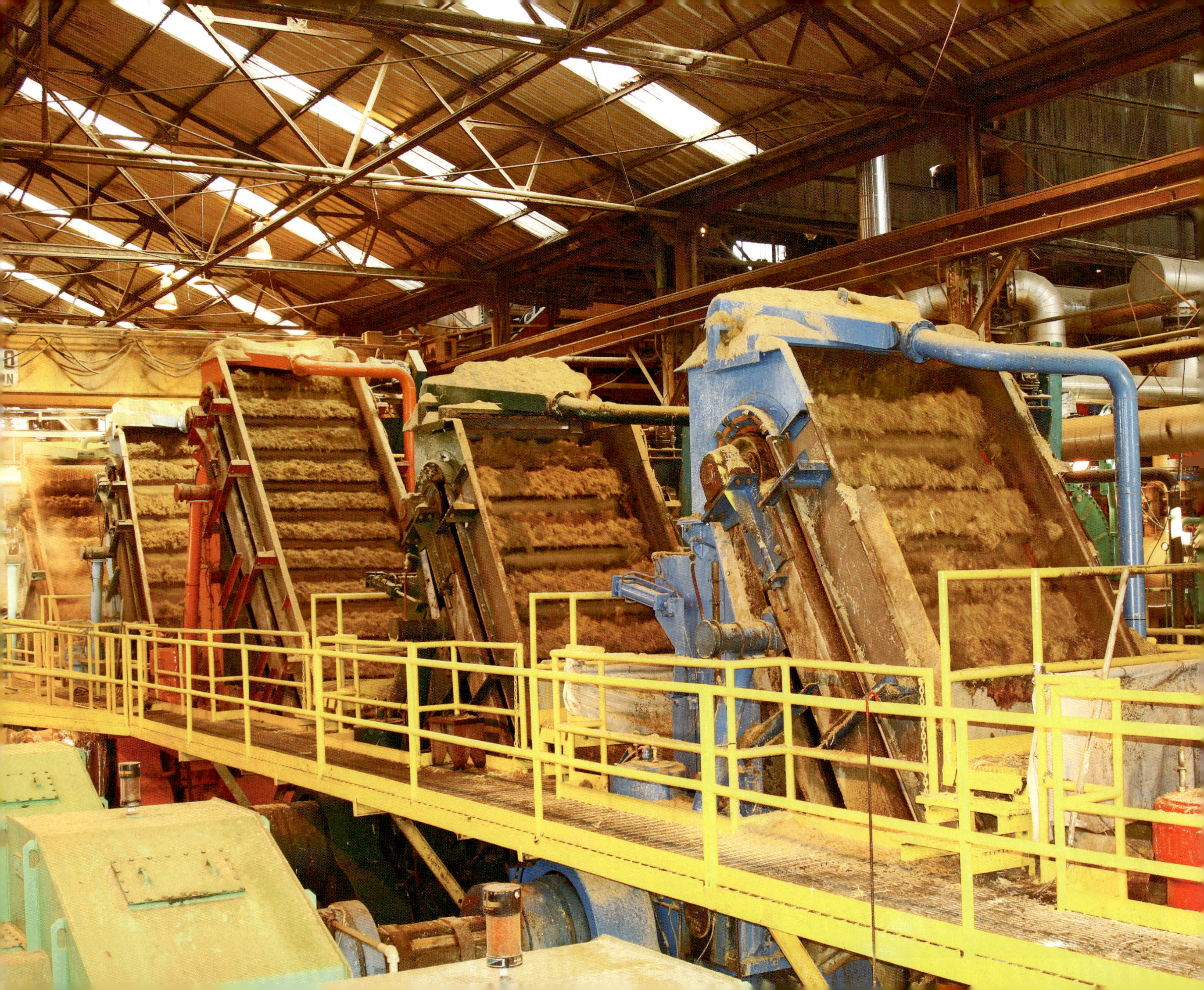

◆ The mill tandem

As the cane is conveyed into the mill on the main cane carrier, it is chopped up with rotating knives and shredded with hammer-like devices. This process renders a uniform mat of mangled cane.

The cane is then conveyed to what is called the mill tandem. A mill is a set of 4 or 5 rollers that squeeze the juice from the cane. A mill tandem is a series of 5 or 6 such mills, one feeding the cane into the next, with the rollers squeezing tighter and tighter as the cane proceeds through the mills.

The prepared cane is repeatedly mixed with water or diluted cane juice and crushed between the rollers as it goes from one mill to the next. By the time it gets to the last mill, the maximum amount of juice (about 95%) has been extracted from it. The remaining fibrous content is called bagasse.

Juice is squeezed out of the cane as it goes through the mills. **Facing page:** *Cane moves from one mill to the next in the mill tandem, a series of 5 of 6 mills.* **Right:** *Pulverized cane goes through each mill at a high rate of speed.*

Rollers of a mill squeeze juice out of the cane, separating it from the fibrous pulp.

◆ Bagasse as fuel

Bagasse is sent to the boilers to be used as fuel and burned to create energy. These boilers produce steam to run turbines within the mill, as well as generators, to produce electricity.

Bagasse – the fibrous, bulky material left over after the juice has been squeezed from the sugarcane – is used as fuel to create energy for use in the mill. **Above:** *An ash-puller removes bagasse ash from a boiler.* **Right:** *Flames and sparks shoot out from behind the boiler door.*

◆ Juice heaters

The juice from the mills is sent to the juice heaters, where it is heated and mixed with lime to adjust its pH level to 7. The lime helps to remove any remaining impurities. The liming can be done prior to or after heating the juice.

◆ Juice clarifier

The heated juice is sent to a clarifier to settle out any traces of mud and thereby to yield the clearest juice possible.

◆ Mud filters

The mud that is separated out by the clarifier is sent to mud filters in order to recover the remaining juice with the help of a vacuum. The leftover mud is sent to the mud pits and eventually returned to the fields.

A mill worker helps to remove mud from a mud filter. The mud is scraped off and drops into a trough before being brought outdoors to a mud pit or to the mill pond.

◆ Evaporator stations

The clarified juice goes to the evaporator stations, where evaporators remove most of the water from the juice, resulting in a thicker syrup.

◆ Crystallization in the vacuum pans

The syrup is sent to closed cylindrical vessels called vacuum pans, where the process of crystallization of the sugar begins. The syrup is boiled in these pans at a low temperature and under vacuum. It is cooked down until it reaches the supersaturation stage.

At this point, small sugar crystals are introduced into the syrup and they grow to commercial sugar size. This process of "growing" crystals by boiling them with the syrup is called crystallization. When the desired crystal size is reached, the mixture is called *massecuite*.

Vacuum pans are where the critical process of crystallization of sugar is initiated.

Louisiana Sugarcane Pictorial 55

Massecuite is thick cane syrup containing commercial-size crystals. At this stage, the product is only one step away from becoming raw sugar.

Mill workers examine the size of sugar crystals contained in cane syrup known as massecuite. When the crystals have grown to a certain size, it's time to move the massecuite to the next phase of sugar production.

◆ Centrifugals

The *massecuite* from the vacuum pans enters a holding tank called a mixer; the mixer includes slow-moving paddles that prevent the sugar crystals from settling.

The *massecuite* is then transferred to high-speed machines called centrifugals – which are a lot like washing machines.

The *massecuite* is spun like wet clothes in an ordinary washing machine. In the process, the molasses separates out like water from the clothes in the final spin-dry cycle. The sugar is like the clothes in the washer: It collects on the perimeter of the tub.

Then the sugar is scraped off, dried and sent by conveyor belts to the sugar warehouse.

Centrifugals are like high-speed washing machines in a spin-dry cycle, spinning the massecuite and separating the raw sugar from the molasses.

◆ **The sugar warehouse**

Raw sugar is moved to the warehouse by conveyor belt, and near the end of its journey it is slung into a huge pile by a sugar slinger.

Raw sugar from the centrifugals arrives in the sugar warehouse on a conveyor belt and is slung into a pile by a sugar slinger.

A tall pile of raw sugar keeps getting taller as a sugar slinger adds to its height.

◆ **Transporting raw sugar to the refinery**

Raw sugar is taken from the warehouse and shipped to a refinery by barge, truck or railcar.

Trucks bound for a refinery are filled with raw sugar by a front-end loader.

Raw sugar is loaded onto a barge bound for a refinery.

Tugboat pushes a sugar barge on Bayou Teche from Cajun Sugar Co-op in New Iberia.

60 *Louisiana Sugarcane Pictorial*

Lousiana Sugar Refining, Gramercy, La.

1. Mixing vats are used to mix warm, sweet water and steam with raw sugar, to aid in the removal of molasses. The resulting mixture is called magma.

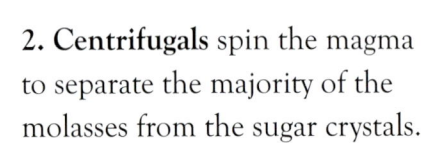

2. Centrifugals spin the magma to separate the majority of the molasses from the sugar crystals.

Chapter 5
The refining process

When raw sugar is delivered from the mill to the refinery for further processing, it is said to be "unrefined" because it still contains molasses and traces of impurities.

The refinement process is designed to rid the sugar of these elements and to yield the purest, whitest sugar possible.

Numerous steps are taken to reach this goal, beginning with the removal of the molasses and various impurities and ending with the sorting and bagging of the end product according to the size of the sugar crystals.

3. Clarifiers – The sugar crystals are washed, dissolved, clarified and filtered to remove the last traces of molasses and any insoluble impurities. The resulting product is a clear, golden liquid.

4. Deep-bed filters are used to remove the leftover impurities.

5. Decolorizer eliminates the remaining color and any last traces of impurities, producing a syrup composed of water and white sugar.

6. Evaporators remove water from the product and yield a more concentrated syrup.

7. Vacuum pans – The syrup is fed into vacuum pans, where it is seeded with sugar crystals. The crystals then proceed to grow to the desired size.

8. Centrifugals spin and wash the thick syrup with hot water, separating the sugar crystals from the remaining liquid.

9. Driers reduce the moisture content of the sugar crystals to .03%.

10. Sorters – Sugar moves through a machine with a graduated series of fine-mesh screens that vibrate as they separate crystals according to size. (Different customers require different size crystals.)

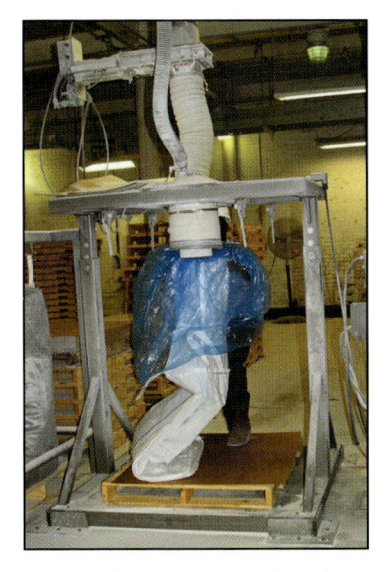

11. Packaging – Refined sugar is stored temporarily in huge plastic bags called "totes." It is then packaged in various size bags to send to consumers, packagers or food-processing companies.

12. Transporting – Packaged sugar is shipped from the refinery usually by truck. Bulk sugar (unpackaged) is loaded onto rail cars and shipped to food-processing companies that make cakes, candies, cereals and the like.

Chapter 6

South Louisiana's sugar mills

At the turn of the 20th century, hundreds of small sugar mills were in operation in Louisiana, most in the southern part of the state.

But that number dwindled in the 1920s and '30s due to disease, adverse weather including hurricanes, financial catastrophe caused by the Great Depression, and inefficiencies of various kinds. Only the strongest survived.

By the 1960s, approximately 45 to 50 mills were still in operation; that number stood at 11 in 2014. The mills today are large, efficient and technologically advanced. They operate around-the-clock during grinding season. They have the capacity to process huge amounts of sugarcane, some mills as much as 2 million tons or even more per season.

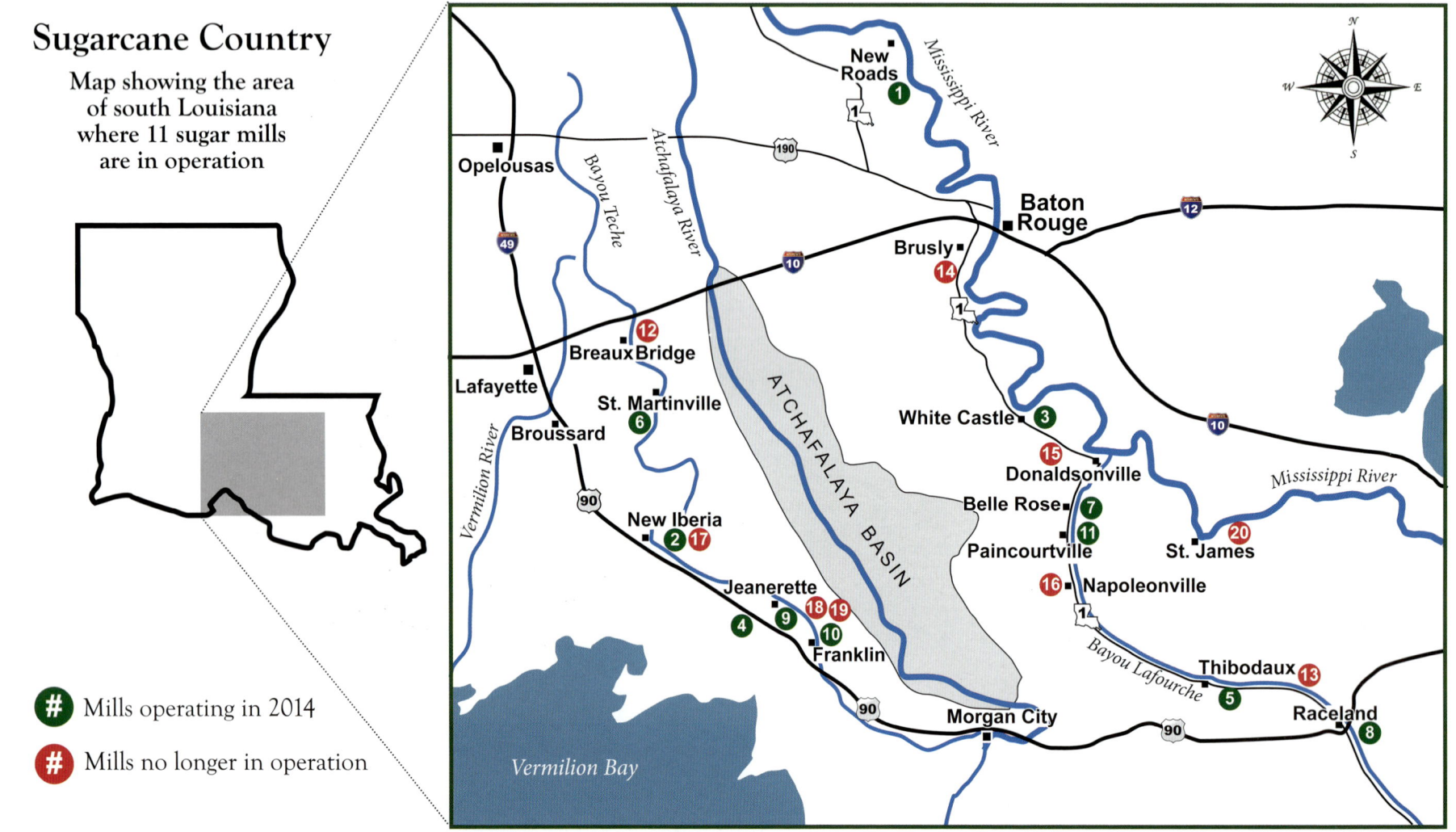

Sugarcane Country

Map showing the area of south Louisiana where 11 sugar mills are in operation

- ⑨ Mills operating in 2014
- ⑨ Mills no longer in operation

- Map work by Robert Clements

Louisiana Sugarcane Pictorial **67**

Alma Plantation, LLC
Lakeland • Est. 1846

68 *Louisiana Sugarcane Pictorial*

Cajun Sugar Cooperative, Inc.
New Iberia • Est. 1964

Cora Texas Factory
White Castle • Est. 1927

Enterprise Factory
(M.A. Patout & Sons)
Patoutville • Est. 1825

Louisiana Sugarcane Pictorial **71**

Lafourche Sugars, LLC
Thibodaux • Est. 1937

Louisiana Sugar Cane Co-op, Inc.
St. Martinville • Est. 1870

Lula Sugar Factory
Belle Rose • Est. 1900

Raceland Raw Sugar Corp.
Raceland • Est. 1892

St. Mary Sugar Co-op, Inc.
Jeanerette • Est. 1946

76 *Louisiana Sugarcane Pictorial*

Sterling Sugars, Inc.
Franklin • Est. 1807

Westfield Sugar Factory
Paincourtville • Est. 1890

Breaux Bridge Sugar Co-op
Breaux Bridge • 1938 – 1997

Caldwell Sugar Co-op
Thibodaux • 1946 – 2001

Cinclare Sugar Mill
(Harry L. Laws & Co.)
Brusly • 1878 – 2005

Evan Hall Sugar Mill
Donaldsonville • 1936 – 2000

Glenwood Sugar Mill
Napoleonville • 1933 – 2002

Iberia Sugar Cooperative
New Iberia • 1937 – 2004

Jeanerette Sugar Co-op
Jeanerette • 1937 – 2004

Louisiana Sugarcane Pictorial **85**

– Photo by Ory Miguez, Courtesy of Miguez Studio, Franklin, La.

Oaklawn Sugar Mill
Franklin • 1837 – 1990

St. James Sugar Mill
St. James • 1947 – 2006

Chapter 7

Images of the past

While the sugarcane business today employs modern techniques and the latest in farming and milling equipment, remnants of its past can be seen scattered about the landscape of south Louisiana.

Off the beaten path, one can find derricks that haven't been used for decades, ancient tractors that died of old age a long time ago, and skeletons of long-abandoned sugar factories and syrup mills.

An abandoned, weather-beaten syrup mill in Rosedale...

Meeker Sugar Cooperative, located near Lecompte in central Louisiana, opened in 1912 and operated for nearly seven decades before closing in 1981. The facility was added to the National Register of Historic Places in 1987.

This old mill tandem at St. Mary Sugar Co-op in Jeanerette was replaced with a more modern version in the late 1980s.

*The cane yard of Jeanerette Sugar Co-op as it appeared in the mid-1990s...
The mill was in operation 67 years before closing in 2004.*

Louisiana Sugarcane Pictorial **91**

The remains of an old sugar mill near Jeanerette...

This cane derrick on a farm near Paincourtville is no longer in use. In the past, it was used to lift cane from a cart that mules pulled from the fields, then it placed the cane in another cart that a tractor hauled to the mill.

Chapter 8

Parting shots

Both the farming and milling aspects of the sugarcane business provide an abundance of potential for good pictures of an industry that is a vital part of Louisiana's modern-day economy.

These photographic opportunities include the interiors of sugar mills illuminated by strong beams of light, cane fields on fire during the fall harvest, and tractors hauling cane over roads framed by moss-draped oaks.

"Stairway to Heaven" – Sunshine lights the stairway in the lab area of Westfield Sugar Factory at Paincourtville.

Louisiana Sugarcane Pictorial 93

*The boiler room of St. Mary Sugar Co-op in Jeanerette is well-lighted in mid-morning.
(A 30-second exposure was used to capture this special effect.)*

Louisiana sugar mills are major operations that process tremendous amounts of cane each season. **Left:** A giant grab moves a load of cane from the cane yard to the cane table, where it will be conveyed into the mill for processing. This picture was taken at Lafourche Sugars in Thibodaux. **Facing page:** Pulverized cane runs through the mill tandem, where the juice is squeezed out between large rollers. The photo was taken at Louisiana Sugar Cane Co-op in St. Martinville.

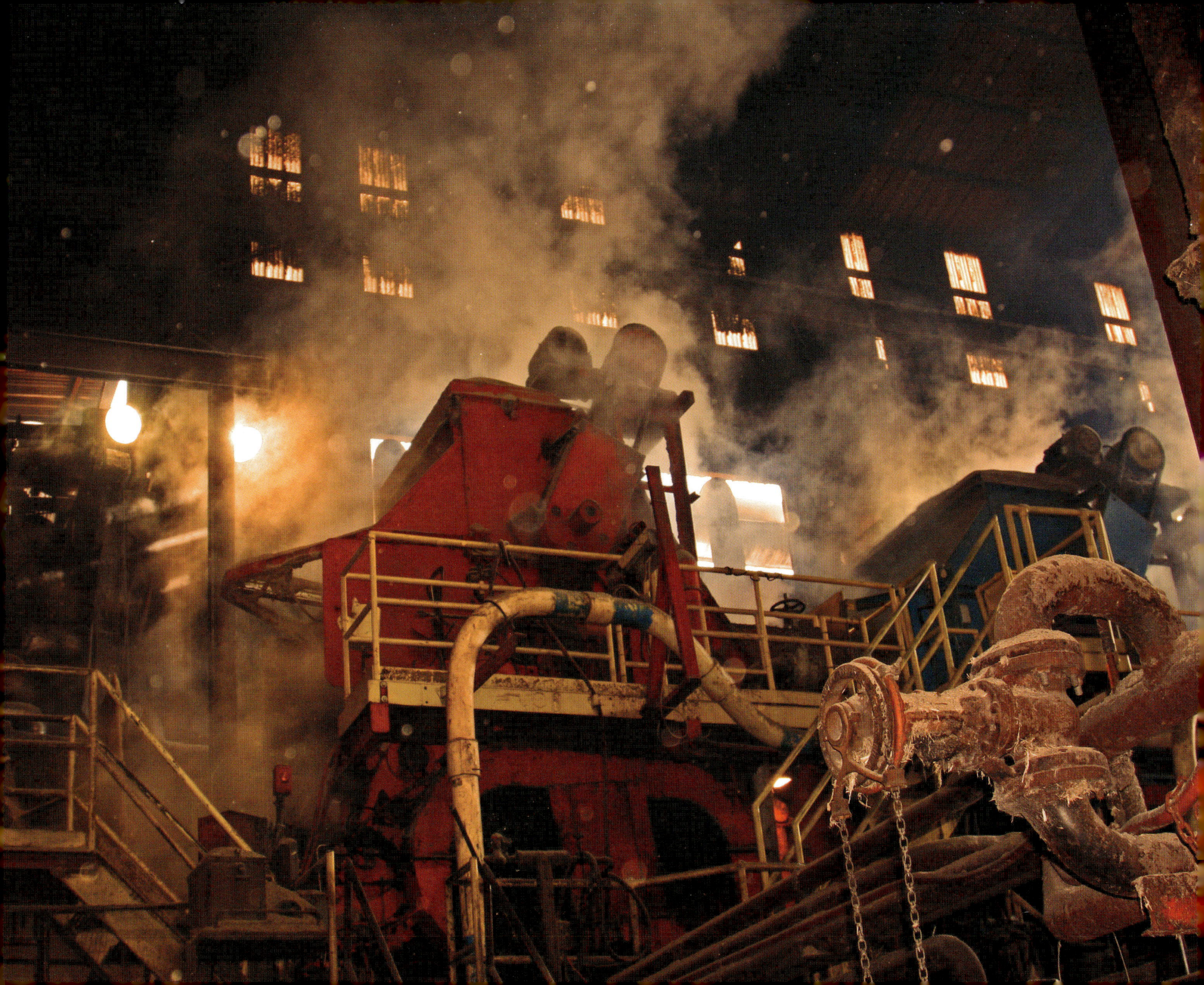

A crown wheel is heated as it is attached to the shaft of a large roller. The crown wheel turns the roller, which is part of the apparatus that squeezes juice from the sugarcane.

A mill worker stokes the flames in a boiler at Sterling Sugars in Franklin. The fuel for this fire is sugarcane bagasse, the highly fibrous by-product left over from the cane after the juice has been extracted.

98 *Louisiana Sugarcane Pictorial*

A colorful array of mechanical sugarcane planters, near the M. A. Patout Mill in Patoutville...

Cane is loaded into carts bound for St. Mary Sugar Co-op in Jeanerette.

Smoke from boilers billows from smoke stacks at Iberia Sugar Cooperative in New Iberia. The mill was in operation from 1937 to 2004.

Louisiana Sugarcane Pictorial 101

A derrick and a gigantic grab are part of the tools of the trade that were used to move sugarcane at Jeanerette Sugar Co-op in its heyday.

Shafts of strong morning light stream in to the central work area of Moresi Foundry in Jeanerette. The foundry has serviced the needs of sugar mills in Louisiana and elsewhere since 1885.

Sunlight illuminates the mill tandem of Raceland Raw Sugar Corp. at Raceland.

104 *Louisiana Sugarcane Pictorial*

Cane is cut in the Franklin area by a single-row harvester operated by farmer Jessie Breaux.

Louisiana Sugarcane Pictorial **105**

A loader moves cane stalks into a cane truck circa 1988.

106 *Louisiana Sugarcane Pictorial*

A tractor pulls carts of cane to Louisiana Sugar Cane Co-op in St. Martinville.

Sun sets behind a south Louisiana sugarcane field.

INDEX

Note: Page numbers in *italics* indicate photographs, maps, or content within the captions of photographs.

Alma Plantation, *67*
airplanes, 23, 29, *29*
area map, *66*
ash-puller, *51*

Bagasse, 49, 51, *51*, *97*
billet cane planter, 25
billet harvester, 5, 12, *13*, 25, 31, *31*, *32*
billets, 25, 31
boilers, 51, *51*, *93*, *97*, *100*
Breaux, Jessie, *104*
Breaux Bridge Sugar Co-op, *78*
burning cane fields, 5, 12, *13*, 31, *34*, *36*, *37*

Cajun Sugar Cooperative, *59*, *68*
Caldwell Sugar Co-op, *79*
carts, 5, 6, 15, *37*, *38*, *39*, *40*, *41*, *42*, *42*, *43*, *44*, *44*, *91*, *99*, *106*
centrifugals, 43, 56, *56*, *57*, *60*, *63*
Cinclare Sugar Mill, *80*
clarifiers, 53, 61
cleaning, 6, 7, *11*
conveyors, 43, *45*, *46*, 49, *56*, 57
Cora Texas Factory, *69*
crop rotation, 18
crown wheel, *96*

crystallization, 5, 54, *54*
crystals (sugar), 54, *55*, 56, *60*, 61, 63, 64
cultivation, 5, 18, 20

De Boré, Etienne, 5
decolorizer, 62
deep-bed filters, 61
derrick, 87, *91*, *101*
drainage, 7, *12*
driers, 64

Economy, 6, *92*
eighteen-wheelers, 31, *38*, 40
end-dumping, 44, *45*
Enterprise Factory, 70
Evan Hall Sugar Mill, *81*
evaporator stations, 53
evaporators, 62

Farmers, 5, 6, 7, 18, *19*, 25, 26, *34*, 43, *104*
fertilizer, 5, 15, *17*
front-end loader, 46, 47, *59*
fungicides, 15

Glenwood Sugar Mill, *82*
grab, 46, *94*, *101*
grinding season, 5, 7, *10*, *11*, 66

Harvest season, 5, 7, 12, *13*, 15, 29
harvesting, 5, 6, 7, 8, *12*, *13*, 18, 25, 29, 31
headlands, 7, *12*
heat-treat, 26
helicopters, 23, 29
herbicides, 15, *15*, 20, 22, 23

Iberia Sugar Cooperative, *83*, *100*
insecticides, 15, *23*

Jeanerette Sugar Co-op, *84*, *90*, *101*
juice clarifier, 52
juice heaters, 52
juice, 5, 43, 49, *49*, 50, 51, 52, 53, *94*, *96*, *97*

Lafourche Sugars, *71*, *94*
liming, 52
loader, *38*, *105*
Louisiana Sugar Cane Co-op, *72*, *94*, *106*

Louisiana Sugar Cane Festival, 6
Louisiana Sugar Refining, *60*
Lula Sugar Factory, *73*

M.A. Patout Mill, *70*, *98*
magma, 60
maintenance, 7
map of Sugarcane Country, *66*
massecuite, 54, *55*, 56, *56*
Meeker Sugar Cooperative, *88*
mill tandem, 49, *49*, *89*, *94*, *103*
mill workers, *53*, *55*, *97*
millers, 5, 7
milling process, 10, 12, 43
mills, 5, 7, 42, 43, *43*, 44, *44*, 46, 47, 49, *49*, 51, *51*, 52, 54, *87*, *91*, *94*, *100*, *102*
mixer, 56
mixing vats, 60
Moresi Foundry, *102*
mud, 43, 44, *44*, 52, 53
mud filters, 53

National Register of Historic Places, *88*

Oaklawn Sugar Mill, *85*

off-barring, *16*
offloading, 5, *42*, 43, 44

Packaging, 65
packer, 26, *26*
planters, 25, *98*
planting, 5, *25-28*

Raceland Raw Sugar Corp., *74*, *103*
raw sugar, 5, 43, *55*, 56, *57*, *57*, 58, *59*, *59*, 60, 61, *61*, 63
refinery, 5, 59, *59*, 61
refining process, 61
repairing, 6, 7, *11*
ripener, 29, *29*
rollers, *11*, 43, 49, *50*, *94*, *96*

Sampling cane , 42
"soldier" harvesters, 25, *32*
sorghum, *18*
sorters, 64
soybeans, 18, *19*
St. James Sugar Mill, *86*
St. Mary Sugar Co-op, *75*, *89*, *93*, *99*
Sterling Sugars, *76*, *97*
sucrose content, *43*

sugar, 5, 31, 43, 54, *55*, 56, *57*, *58*, *59*, 60, 61, 62, 64, 65
Sugar Bowl, 6
sugar crystals, 54, *55*, 56, 60, 61, *63*
sugar warehouse, 56, 57, *57*, *59*
sugar slinger, 57, *57*, *58*
sugarcane mills, 5, 6, 7, 66, *67-86*, *91*, *92*, *94*, *97*, *102*
syrup, 53, 54, *55*, 62, *63*

Testing, 43
tilling, 20
tractors, 5, 6, 9, *12*, *15*, 26, 31, *39*, *41*, 44, *87*, *91*, *92*, *106*
trailers, 6, 8, *45*
transporting, 59, 65
trucks, 5, 42, *42*, 43, 44, *45*, 59, *59*, 65, *105*

Vacuum pans, 54, *54*, 56, *63*

Warehouse, sugar, 56, 57, *57*, *59*
weighing, *42*
welders, *11*
Westfield Sugar Factory, *77*, *92*
wheat, 18, *18*

whole-stalk cane, 12, *13*, 24, 25, 27, 31, *34*, *37*
whole-stalk harvester, 5, *13*, 31, *32*
whole-stalk planter, 26, 27

Acknowledgments

I acknowledge with gratitude the sugarcane industry experts who reviewed this book in advance and suggested ways to make it as accurate as possible. These include:

- Harold Birkett, associate professor, LSU Agricultural Center, Audubon Sugar Institute in Baton Rouge.
- Jessie Breaux Jr., career sugarcane farmer and resident of Franklin, La.
- Mike Comb, plant manager of Louisiana Sugar Cane Co-op in St. Martinville, La.
- Larry Faucheux, CEO and general manager of Louisiana Sugar Refining in Gramercy, La.
- Ken Gravois, sugarcane specialist with the LSU Agricultural Center's Sugar Research Station at St. Gabriel, La.
- Don Lilleboe, editor and general manager of Sugar Publications in Fargo, N.D., and publisher of *U.S. Sugar Industry Directory*.

Also, I am grateful to the staff of Acadian House Publishing, who worked diligently to help assure this book would be the well-organized, first-class product that I envisioned when I decided to go forward with the project. These include Trent Angers, editor and publisher; Charlotte Huggins, who produced the interior pages of the book; Bob Clements, who put together the map locating all the mills in operation in Louisiana today; and Darlene Smith, who went above and beyond the call of duty in proofreading and fact-checking the manuscript. I'd also like to recognize graphic artist Glenn Noya of New Orleans for his meticulous work in designing and producing the covers.

Photographic Prints of the Sugarcane Industry *By Ronnie Olivier* **Available Now**

An extensive collection of photos of the sugarcane industry – including some of the pictures in this book – plus several other subjects can be viewed and purchased at reasonable rates at this website:

cajunphotography.artistwebsites.com

About the Photographer / Author...

RONNIE OLIVIER is an award-winning photographer and safety engineer for the sugar industry, operating as Louisiana Safety Consultants, Inc.

He graduated from the University of Southwestern Louisiana in Lafayette in 1974 with a degree in industrial engineering and worked for Avondale Shipyards in Morgan City, La., then for J. Ray McDermott as a safety engineer and photographer. From 1985 to 1989 he worked for International Salt Mine at Avery Island, La., after which he began working as a safety engineer for the sugar industry.

He served in the U.S. Army for two years in the early 1970s, including a tour of duty in Korea. He photographed Little League baseball and youth football in New Iberia, La., for about 15 years, beginning in 1974. He has done job-related photography continuously since 1974.

His photographs have been published in numerous sugar industry journals as well as local and regional publications.

He and his wife, May, live in Lafayette.

Getting into photography...

When I was a youngster I watched my dad and my uncle when they came home from a photo shoot and developed the pictures they had taken.

They took great pride in their work. After developing their film and printing their pictures they would take tooth picks and attach cotton to the ends and hand-paint the pictures to match the colors of the clothing of their subjects. Mostly they shot weddings and portraits.

As I got older, my dad allowed me to go with him and help when he photographed weddings. When I was in the service and stationed in Korea in the early 1970s, there was very little to do with my free time, so I bought a 35 mm camera and started taking pictures, more particularly slides. A slide cost a few pennies in Korea.

When I returned home I started taking pictures for football and baseball youth leagues. I also became the official photographer at most of the places where I worked.

Today I carry my camera almost everywhere I go. I really enjoy capturing an idea or a feeling with the camera. And I must say I owe my interest in photography to my dad, Henry J. Olivier Jr., and my uncle, Marion Olivier.

Regional Books About Intriguing South Louisiana

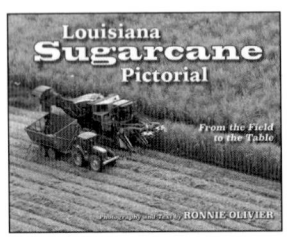

Louisiana Sugarcane Pictorial
From the Field to the Table

A 112-page hardcover book of top-notch photographs depicting virtually every aspect of the south Louisiana sugarcane industry – from planting and harvesting the crop to milling and refining the cane. Also featured are aerial photos of all 11 mills operating in this region, as well as rare pictures of old machinery and buildings that served the industry in a bygone era. (Photographer/Author: Ronnie Olivier. ISBN: 0-925417-93-9. Price $34.95)

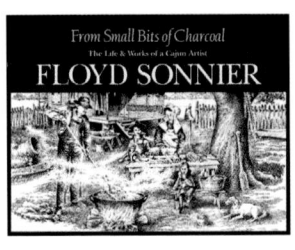

From Small Bits Of Charcoal:
The Life & Works of a Cajun Artist

This 190-page hardcover book is the autobiography of pen-and-ink artist Floyd Sonnier (1933-2002) of Lafayette, La. Written and illustrated by Mr. Sonnier, the book tells the story of growing up as a French-speaking Cajun in rural south Louisiana in the 1940s and '50s. It is a testament to his love of his French-Acadian, or Cajun, culture and heritage. (Author & Artist: Floyd Sonnier. ISBN: 0-925417-46-7. Price: $59.95)

The Nature Of Things At LAKE MARTIN
Exploring the wonders of Cypress Island Preserve in southern Louisiana

A 128-page hardcover book describing the 9,300-acre preserve that includes one of the most impressive wading bird rookeries in North America. Beautifully illustrated with photographs of birds, alligators, furry animals and people who live here, as well as pictures of the woods and waters of the area. The book has two maps, lists of the 200-plus birds that have been seen here, and tips on photographing birds and other animals. (Photographer/Author: Nancy Camel. ISBN: 0-925417-54-8. Price: $44.95)

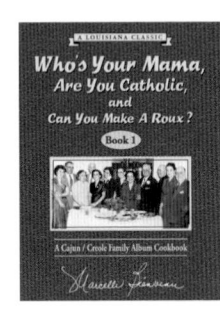

Who's Your Mama, Are You Catholic, And Can You Make A Roux?

A 160-page hardcover book containing more than 200 Cajun and Creole recipes, plus old photos and interesting stories about the author's growing up in the Cajun country of south Louisiana. Recipes include Pain Perdu, Couche Couche, Chicken Fricassée, Stuffed Mirliton, Shrimp Stew, Grillades, Red Beans & Rice, Shrimp Creole, Bouillabaisse, Pralines. (Author: Marcelle Bienvenu. ISBN: 0-925417-55-6. Price: $22.95)

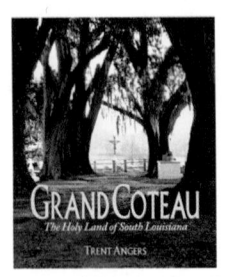

Grand Coteau
The Holy Land of South Louisiana

A 176-page hardcover book that captures the spirit of one of the truly holy places in North America. It is a town of mystery, with well-established ties to the supernatural, including the famous Miracle of Grand Coteau. Brought to life by dozens of exceptional color photographs, the book focuses on the town's major religious institutions: The Academy of the Sacred Heart, Our Lady of the Oaks Retreat House and St. Charles College/Jesuit Spirituality Center. The book explores not only the history of these three institutions but also the substance of their teachings. (Author: Trent Angers. ISBN: 0-925417-47-5. Price: $44.95)

Blessed Be Jazz
The Story of My Life as a Clarinet-Playing Jesuit Priest in the French Quarter of New Orleans

The 192-page hardcover autobiography of Rev. Frank Coco, SJ (1920-2006), a Jesuit priest who served for more than 50 years in south Louisiana as a retreat director, high school teacher and jazz musician. Using his clarinet, he performed extensively in New Orleans nightclubs, sitting in with some of the best-known jazz musicians of his time, including Ronnie Kole, Al Hirt and Pete Fountain. (Author: Fr. Frank Coco, SJ. ISBN: 0-925417-89-0. Price: $19.95)

TO ORDER, list the books you wish to purchase along with the corresponding cost of each. Add shipping & handling cost of $4 for the first book and $1 per book thereafter. Louisiana residents add 8% tax to the cost of the books. Mail your order and check or credit card authorization (VISA/MC/AmEx) to: Acadian House Publishing, Dept. SGR, P.O. Box 52247, Lafayette, LA 70505. Or call (800) 850-8851. To order online, go to www.acadianhouse.com.